Book of Saints

"SUPER-HEROES OF GOD"

By REV. LAWRENCE G. LOVASIK, S.V.D.
Divine Word Missionary

PART 9

D1797350

CONTENTS

NIHIL OBSTAT: Francis J. McAree, S.T.D., *Censor Librorum*
IMPRIMATUR: ✝ Patrick J. Sheridan, D.D.,
Vicar General, Archdiocese of New York

© 1996 by CATHOLIC BOOK PUBLISHING CORP., N.J.
Printed in Hong Kong   ISBN 978-0-89942-504-7
CPSIA   November 2014   10 9 8 7 6 5 4   A/P

Saint Fulgentius of Ruspe

BORN into a noble senatorial family of Carthage, Fabius Claudius Gordianus Fulgentius received an excellent education including Latin and Greek.

He was chosen lieutenant governor of Byzacena. But after reading a sermon of Saint Augustine, he decided to become a monk.

His austere lifestyle attracted many followers and he was elected Bishop of Ruspe (modern Kudiat Rosfa in Tunisia).

Shortly afterward, he was tortured and sent into exile by the Arian king. The Arians were heretics who denied the divinity of Christ. Fulgentius and the other exiles built a monastery and devoted themselves to prayer and study.

When a new king ruled in Carthage, the exiles returned home. Fulgentius won the people over to the true Faith by his powerful preaching and example of humility. He died on January 1, 533.

Although he suffered for the Faith, this holy man remained true. He based his teaching on the writings of Saint Augustine and has been called a "pocket Augustine."

Saint Hildegund

February 6

IT was in Germany in the twelfth century when Hildegund, wife of Count Lothair, was left a widow with young children when he died.

Later one of her sons died and the second son entered a monastery. So Hildegund, uncertain of her future, made a pilgrimage to Rome.

She then turned her efforts to establishing a house of prayer and praise to God. She dedicated all her possessions to Christ and converted her castle into a convent.

Hildegund and her daughter Hedwig assumed the Premonstratensian habit and began a new foundation with Hildegund as prioress. Her kindness and spirit of fervor attracted many others to a life of prayer and good works.

Both Hildegund's daughter Hedwig and her son Herman were known to the people as Blessed. Hildegund died in 1183 with a great reputation for sanctity, especially because of the example she gave in turning away from material possessions to seek only the honor and glory of God.

Saint Miguel Cordero

FRANCISCO Febres Cordero Muñoz was born in 1854 to a prominent family in Ecuador. He was not able to stand till age five. Then he saw a vision of the Blessed Mother and was cured.

He attended a school run by the Christian Brothers, and when he was of age, decided to join their Congregation. He was accepted and became known as Brother Miguel.

Miguel's first assignment was in Quito where he remained for thirty-two years. He was an out-standing teacher and wrote many books on educa-tion. The government of Ecuador adopted his texts for schools throughout the country. In 1892, Brother Miguel was elected to the national Academy of Letters.

Despite his fame in the field of education, Brother Miguel delighted in preparing the very young for their First Holy Communion. He also wrote manuals of piety, gave religious instruction, and conducted retreats.

Miguel died in 1910 in Spain and his body was returned to Ecuador with great public ceremony.

Saint Cuthbert

March 20

ALTHOUGH there is some confusion as to whether Cuthbert was born in Ireland, Scotland, or England, we know that he was orphaned at an early age. For a time he was a shepherd, and eventually became a monk at Melrose Abbey. Shortly afterward, he became the abbot there.

Later Cuthbert, with most of the monks of Lindisfarne, migrated to Ireland. Then he became prior of Lindisfarne or Holy Island. He loved God's creatures and was protector of the seabirds.

Cuthbert was also involved in missionary activities and attracted large crowds by his preaching. Then because of his desire for solitude, he became a hermit living on an island in seclusion.

Against his will Cuthbert was chosen Bishop of Hexam. He arranged to switch Sees and thus became Bishop of Lindisfarne.

The last years of his life were spent in ministering to his flock, caring for the sick, and working numerous healings. Cuthbert died at Lindisfarne in 687.

Saint Benedict the Black

April 4

AS a slave who was given his freedom, Benedict the Black, also known as Benedict the Moor, devoted his life to God. Born near Messina, Italy, in 1526, he became a hermit and later superior of a community of hermits.

When the community was disbanded, Benedict became a Franciscan lay brother at Saint Mary's Convent in Palermo.

At first he served as the cook, and later he was appointed superior. But preferring a life of service, he asked to be relieved of such responsibilities and became the cook again.

Benedict had a reputation for holiness, miracles, and generosity. He was also a skillful counselor, and many people sought his help. He died in 1589 and is the Patron of Blacks in the United States.

Refusing to allow his humble origins to keep him from his life's goal, Benedict pursued God's love and was richly rewarded. And the sting of slavery was turned into the glorious freedom of the children of God.

Saint Louis Mary Grignion de Montfort

April 28

LOUIS Mary Grignion is best known for spreading devotion to the Most Blessed Virgin Mary both through preaching and by the printed word.

He was born to a poor family at Montfort, France in 1673. Educated at the Jesuit College in Rennes, he was ordained a priest.

His first assignment was as chaplain to a hospital at Poitiers. During his stay there, Louis established a new congregation of nuns, the Daughters of Divine Wisdom.

Then Louis went to Rome and Pope Clement XI appointed him missionary apostolic, and he began to preach in Brittany.

His emotional style caused much reaction, but he was successful, especially in furthering devotion to the Most Blessed Virgin Mary through the Rosary. And he wrote a very popular book, *True Devotion to the Blessed Virgin.*

Later Louis founded the Missionaries of the Company of Mary known as the Montfort Fathers, and he died in 1716.

Saint Mariana of Quito

May 26

ATTRACTED to things religious from a very early age, Mariana dedicated herself completely to God.

She was born in Quito, Ecuador in 1618. Her parents were of Spanish nobility, but she was orphaned as a child. Then Mariana was raised with loving care by her sister.

At the age of twelve she became a recluse in her sister's house guided by her confessor a Jesuit priest. Mariana never left that house for the rest of her life, except to go to church.

She ate very little, slept only three hours a night, and spent much time in prayer. Drawing close to God, Mariana had the gifts of prophecy and miracles.

In 1645 when Quito was ravaged by an earthquake and epidemic, she offered herself publicly as a victim for the sins of the people. The quake ended, and as the epidemic began to subside, Mariana fell ill and died on May 26. She is known as the "Lily of Quito."

Saint Juliana Falconieri

June 19

JULIANA was born of a wealthy Florentine family in 1270. When she was very young her father died. She was raised by her mother and an uncle named Alexis who was one of the founders of the Servite Order.

At age fifteen Juliana refused her family's plan for marriage. She became a Servite tertiary and lived at home until her mother died.

Then Juliana gathered together a group of women dedicated to prayer and good works, and she was appointed superior. She is considered to be foundress of the Servite nuns.

She loved to serve the sick and gladly performed the most repulsive duties for them.

Her life was one of great self-denial, humility, and charity. And Juliana had a fervent devotion to the Eucharist.

In her last years Juliana was afflicted with painful diseases which she bore with joy and patience. Her saintly life ended in her convent at Florence in 1341.

Saint Olga

July 11

OLGA, also known as Helga, was born at Pskov, Russia, around 879. She married Igor, Duke of Kiev.

When Igor was assassinated, Olga reacted with vengeance on his murderers, ordering that they be scalded to death. And she had many of their followers put to death.

Then Olga ruled the country as regent for her son Svyastoslav until he came of age.

In 957 Olga became a Christian and was baptized in Constantinople. She was one of the first Russians to be baptized.

Turning from her former ways, she devoted the rest of her life to the spread of Christianity, and she requested missionaries from Emperor Otto I.

In this endeavor she did not achieve great success. Her son, Soyastoslav, did not become a Christian, but her grandson, Saint Vladimir, evangelized Russia and is its Patron Saint. Olga died at Kiev on July 11 at age ninety.

Blessed Titus Brandsma

BORN of a deeply religious family in the Netherlands in 1881, Anno Sjoera Brandsma became a Carmelite priest taking the name Titus.

He traveled widely speaking for many causes. Moreover, Titus was a journalist and author.

In 1935 he wrote a public protest condemning new laws against the Jews. And he said a Catholic newspaper could not accept Nazi propaganda and still be considered Catholic.

The courageous priest refused to hide from the Nazis. He was arrested and sent to the concentration camp at Dachau.

Titus was beaten nearly every day and harassed by the guards.

Soon he became so weak that he was sent to the prison infirmary. On July 26, 1942, he gave his Rosary to his nurse. She was a former Catholic who left the Church. She injected him with poison and he died in minutes.

Years later that nurse returned to the Faith. On her own accord she testified for Titus at the hearing for his canonization.

Saint Peter Julian Eymard

T HE life of Peter Julian Eymard reminds us that all of us urgently need the nourishment of the Most Blessed Sacrament as we make our way on our pilgrimage in this world.

Peter was born in Grenoble, France in 1811. He was ordained a priest, and after five years of pastoral ministry, joined the Marist Fathers. He served as spiritual director of their junior seminary and later as provincial at Lyons.

In 1856 Peter was dispensed from his vows as a Marist and he organized a religious institute of priests dedicated to the Blessed Sacrament. They were engaged in perpetual adoration of and devotion to the Blessed Sacrament.

Peter also founded a congregation of nuns and a priests' Eucharistic league along with the Confraternity of the Blessed Sacrament.

By his writings, and especially by his example, Peter sought to make our Eucharistic Lord better known and loved. His works show that the Eucharistic presence in our lives is a foretaste of our union with the Father. He died in 1888.

Saint Teresa Benedicta of the Cross (Edith Stein)

EDITH Stein, born in 1891 in Breslau, Poland, was the youngest child of a large Jewish family. She had a brilliant mind and became a doctor of philosophy at age twenty-five.

At a friend's house she saw an autobiography of Saint Teresa of Avila. She read it in a single night and soon after was baptized a Catholic.

Eleven years later Edith entered the Carmel at Cologne. She put behind her the years as a renowned scholar to become a simple nun seeking only closer union with God. She is remembered as a very warm and cheerful person.

Because of the situation in Germany Edith, whose name in religion was Teresa Benedicta of the Cross, was sent to the Carmel at Echt, Holland.

When the Nazis conquered Holland, Teresa was arrested because of her Jewish origin. She was sent to the concentration camp at Auschwitz with her sister Rosa who also became a Catholic. They died together in the gas chamber in 1942. Teresa was declared a Saint in 1998.

Saint Hildegard of Bingen

September 17

AFFLICTED with fragile health as a child, Hildegard, who was born in 1098 in Germany, was placed in the care of her aunt, Blessed Jutta.

Jutta had formed a community of nuns and Hildegard joined them. When Jutta died, Hildegard became prioress and moved the convent to Rupertsburg near Bingen.

Hildegard was favored with visions, prophecies, and revelations. At her spiritual director's request they were recorded in a work called *Scivias* (the one who knows the ways of the Lord) and approved by Pope Eugenius III.

Living in a turbulent age, Hildegard used her talents in the quest for true justice and peace. She corresponded with Popes, emperors, kings, and famous clergy.

Huge crowds sought to consult her and she was hailed as a Saint but some said she was a fraud.

This remarkable woman of God died in 1179. Miracles were reported at her tomb and she was proclaimed a Saint by the people.

Saint Galla

GALLA was the daughter of a noble patrician who had been a Roman consul in 485. After he was unjustly executed, she married, but within a year she was left a widow.

Though young and wealthy, Galla was determined not to marry again but to devote herself to Christ.

She joined a group of consecrated women who lived near Saint Peter's Basilica. For many years she served the poor, the sick, and the needy.

In later years Galla was afflicted with cancer of the breast. One night when she was unable to sleep, she saw a vision of Saint Peter.

Peter told her that she would be going home to heaven soon and that her friend Benedicta would follow in thirty days. And this happened just as predicted.

Saint Gregory recorded Galla's vision in his *Dialogues*. Galla died around the year 550.

The letter of Saint Fulgentius *Concerning the State of Widowhood* was probably addressed to Saint Galla.

Saint Agnes of Assisi

November 16

AGNES, born in Assisi in 1197, was the younger sister of Saint Clare. When Saint Francis sent Clare to the Benedictine convent of Sant' Angelo di Panzo, Agnes joined her there. Agnes was only fifteen years old.

Then Francis gave the sisters the Franciscan habit they desired and sent them to San Damiano to follow a life of poverty and penance. This marked the beginning of the Poor Clares.

Agnes led a life of detachment from the world's goods. In this way, she was able to become more absorbed in the life of God. Agnes became abbess of the Poor Clares convent at Monticelli. And later she founded convents at Mantua, Venice, and Padua. And Agnes firmly supported her sister's struggle for complete poverty in their Order.

In August 1253 Agnes went to Assisi to be with Clare in her last hours. Then Agnes died three months later on November 16.

The tomb of Agnes in the church of Santa Chiara at Assisi has been the site of numerous miracles.

Prayer

O GOD,
You have given us the Saints to be
our examples in this life,
our friends in the spirit,
and our helpers in heaven.

As we read the accounts of their holy lives,
teach us to imitate their words and actions,
so that one day we may be united with them
in Your heavenly dwelling.